The Adventures of Buddy the Bloodhound

LaDonna Wilkerson

Copyrights © 2024
All Rights Reserved

DEDICATION

This book is dedicated to my grandchildren: Zoe Grace, Ezekiel "Zeke" Louis, Kooper Calhoun, Zara Joy, Karson Abraham, Emi Raye and Owen Elijah. You are dearly loved. May you have roots to grow and wings to fly.

In loving memory of my grandson, Dade Asher. I will see you again.

Abe, Zac and Caleb – I thank God every day I get to be your Momma. I love you big.

To the love of my life, Ed, thank you for our journey together. Besides the gift of salvation, you have been my greatest gift. And too often, my biggest headache Thank you for the many adventures. The first time I saw you, my heart whispered, "He's the one!"

Acknowledgments

Thank you to Sue Ann Lewis for encouraging me to write this book.

Thank you to Tiffany Hartbarger for saving Buddy's life.

Thank you to Louise George for her editing expertise and for teaching me that we are all meant to fly.

Thank you to Betty White. Your friendship and sisterhood has been one of life's great blessings. Your belief in me has often been the fire that kept me going.

Forward

Buddy was rescued by the American Black and Tan Coonhound Rescue. Approximately 4.1 million dogs are taken to a dog pound, shelter or animal rescue association every year. Foster homes for dogs are desperately needed across the United States. Fostering a dog until he can be adopted means that the dog will have another chance at life. Please consider adopting a dog from your local dog shelter or a rescue organization. For more information about adopting a Coonhound or a Bloodhound, please contact the American Black and Tan Coonhound Rescue at www.coonhoundrescue.com.

"Uva uvam vivendo varia fit"

Our lives are changed by the lives of those around us.

- Larry McMurtry, Lonesome Dove

Used with permission of the American Black and Tan Coonhound Rescue.

My name is Easy Buddy but there has never been anything easy in my life. I do not know where I was born. For the last two years, I have been living in south Texas. The plane was now taking me on a new adventure. I hoped it was going to be a good one.

As the plane lifted off from the airport, I wondered where I was going. I was a sad and scared dog. I had been to many places in my life, but none of them were good. I just hoped wherever I was going, there would be food, a soft place to sleep and someone to love me.

The pilot told the rescue people that he had never seen such a sad dog. They sent a picture of me in the plane to my new foster family.

I have a list of things I do not like. I wanted to discover things I liked. I did not have shelter at my old home. I slept in a fenced area with no way to get out of the weather. I do not like rain. I am afraid of thunder and lightning. It gets really hot in south Texas. Sometimes, I did not have water to drink. I was always hungry. My ears hurt, my eyes were infected, and my belly was full of parasites. Parasites are bugs that can make you sick. As we traveled to their home, I ignored them for over two hours. I wouldn't even take treats. I was scared.

I was found by a rescue organization. They asked the Wilkersons to foster me. When you foster a dog, it means you promise to give it a good home. I lived a long way from them. That's why I was flying!

I was their third rescue dog. They were just going to foster me. It didn't take long before they decided to adopt me. That was my lucky day! When they put me in their car, I remember the lady saying, You are going to live with us now at the farm. We are your new Momma and Daddy. What was a farm? What was a Momma and Daddy? I didn't know, but the way she said it sounded wonderful!

I DECIDED TO CHECK THEM OUT. WHERE WERE WE GOING?!?

When she met me, Momma looked in my face and exclaimed "He has golden eyes." Most Bloodhounds have dark brown or hazel eyes. Mine are amber gold. Momma then told me, "Those eyes are beautiful, but they are sad. Let's see if we can make them happy!" I was all for that!

The farm is a big place. There is a white house, a red barn and a tan bunkhouse. All the roofs are the same gray color.

There is a dark brown dog. Her name is Scout. She is a Chocolate Labrador. Scout is older than me. She has lived all her life at the farm. She was Momma's dog but spent most of her time in the barn with Daddy or riding the tractor with him.

Scout loved Momma, too. They had a special way of talking. Mom could say just one word, and Scout knew what to do. Momma said she was voice-trained. Scout rarely got in trouble.

I caused enough trouble for both of us!

Besides Scout, there were cows and all kinds of animals. There were armadillos, possums, raccoons, rabbits, skunks and porcupines. Momma did not like armadillos because they dug up her gardens.

The first time I met a porcupine, Momma and Daddy removed the quills from my nose. They snipped the ends of the quills off and pulled them out. I cried a little. Daddy told Momma he hoped I learned my lesson. I didn't.

I wrestled with that porcupine two more times. I had to visit the veterinarian both times. Once, I had to stay all day. It took that long for them to get all of the quills out of my skin. I run from them now!

Momma tried to teach me not to kill the possums. She said they were our helpers. Possums eat ticks and bugs. All I know is that Momma and Daddy let me live here. Those animals are not supposed to be on my farm.

Daddy said that my big nose often got me in trouble. If I smelled something, I would keep smelling and running until I was too tired to run anymore. One time, I ran away from the farm and was gone for three days.

My family looked everywhere for me. Momma called all of the neighbors. She called all the local dog catchers. They walked the farm thinking I might be hurt. I finally found my way back home. Momma and Daddy were so glad to see me.

Another time, I ran across four miles of pasture to the little town nearby. I was so tired I fell asleep on a stranger's porch. He told his neighbors he was going to take me to the country. He was afraid I was going to eat his chickens and goats. One of Momma's friends called and told her where I was. When they came to get me, my friend Tiffany had me on a leash waiting for them. Momma told Daddy that Tiffany had saved my life. I am so glad she did! I never went to that town again!

I sometimes run off when it is time to go in the pen at night. Momma and Daddy put me and Scout in a pen at night because there are coyotes and feral hogs on the farm. One night, just as we got to the gate, I veered off to the west and ran fast. Momma called and called. I kept running.

Later that night, I ran back to the house as fast as I could. I barked until they came out to see me. I was whimpering and walking in circles. I kept walking round and round. "Something scared him," Daddy said. I wanted to tell them what chased me, but I didn't know how. Momma sat with me on the floor of the laundry room until I calmed down. She let me sleep in the laundry basket. It is one of my favorite places to sleep.

I stay close to home after that night.

Sometimes, they talked about how bad I smelled. When I got to the farm I wanted to go everywhere! I would go to the creek and come back wet and dirty. I ran to the pasture and rolled in the hay left by the cattle. I like to chase skunks. They sprayed me five times. I finally stopped chasing them after they sprayed me in the face. It made my eyes burn. I try to get under a storage container where the rabbits live. I dig in the mud. One of them would say to the other "What did he get in this time?"

MOMMA SAYS I SMELL BAD. I CAN'T GO IN THE HOUSE BUT I CAN SURE TRY!

Daddy often gave us a bath in the yard by the bunkhouse. Scout hated baths and would try to run away. Daddy would sternly say, "Stand still." She did.

I love baths. Sitting alone in a pen for two years with no one touching you made baths a joy. I would stand very quietly as the soap suds and water cascaded off of my body. Daddy's hands were big hands, covered with nicks and bruises from farm work. They were always gentle when touching me. I felt something I had never felt before. How I smelled never bothered me. But I gratefully stood for baths if it meant Daddy was scrubbing me.

If they forget to lock the patio doors, I press down on the handle with my big nose and go in the house. Momma finds me asleep in the office on the blue rug. I feel safe there.

If the door is locked, I knock on the door with my paw until they let me in.

Momma always said, "You are a good boy." She said it so many times I began to believe it. Because she told me I really wanted to be. But sometimes I got in trouble. Scout and I like to run down to the big pond and swim. We would jump in, splashing water everywhere. If the cattle are there drinking, they don't like it. Sometimes it makes the cattle run. We do it anyway.

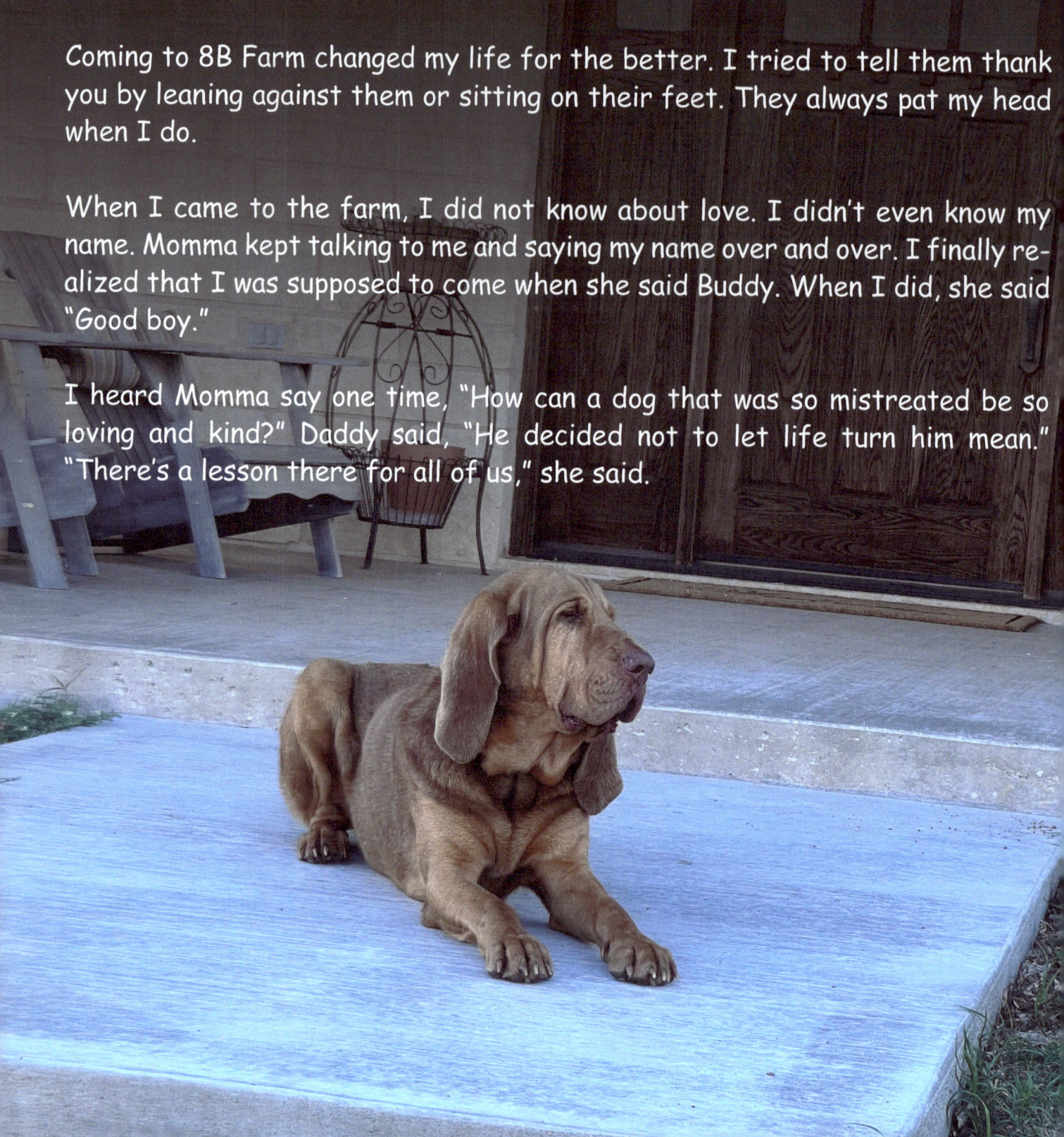

Coming to 8B Farm changed my life for the better. I tried to tell them thank you by leaning against them or sitting on their feet. They always pat my head when I do.

When I came to the farm, I did not know about love. I didn't even know my name. Momma kept talking to me and saying my name over and over. I finally realized that I was supposed to come when she said Buddy. When I did, she said "Good boy."

I heard Momma say one time, "How can a dog that was so mistreated be so loving and kind?" Daddy said, "He decided not to let life turn him mean." "There's a lesson there for all of us," she said.

Being hungry all my life, food was special to me. I always looked Momma and Daddy in the face when they were feeding me. I wanted them to know I was thanking them. I heard Momma and Daddy say thanks all the time. I sure was thankful to know them and Scout. Momma liked the rain. It helped her garden grow and kept the fruit trees alive. She sometimes went out on the back porch holding her arms to the sky and saying loudly, "Thank you, Lord, for the rain." I didn't know why she loved rain, but I was happy to sit by her as she listened to it fall. Scout and I would curl up around her feet as the raindrops hit the metal roof of the farmhouse

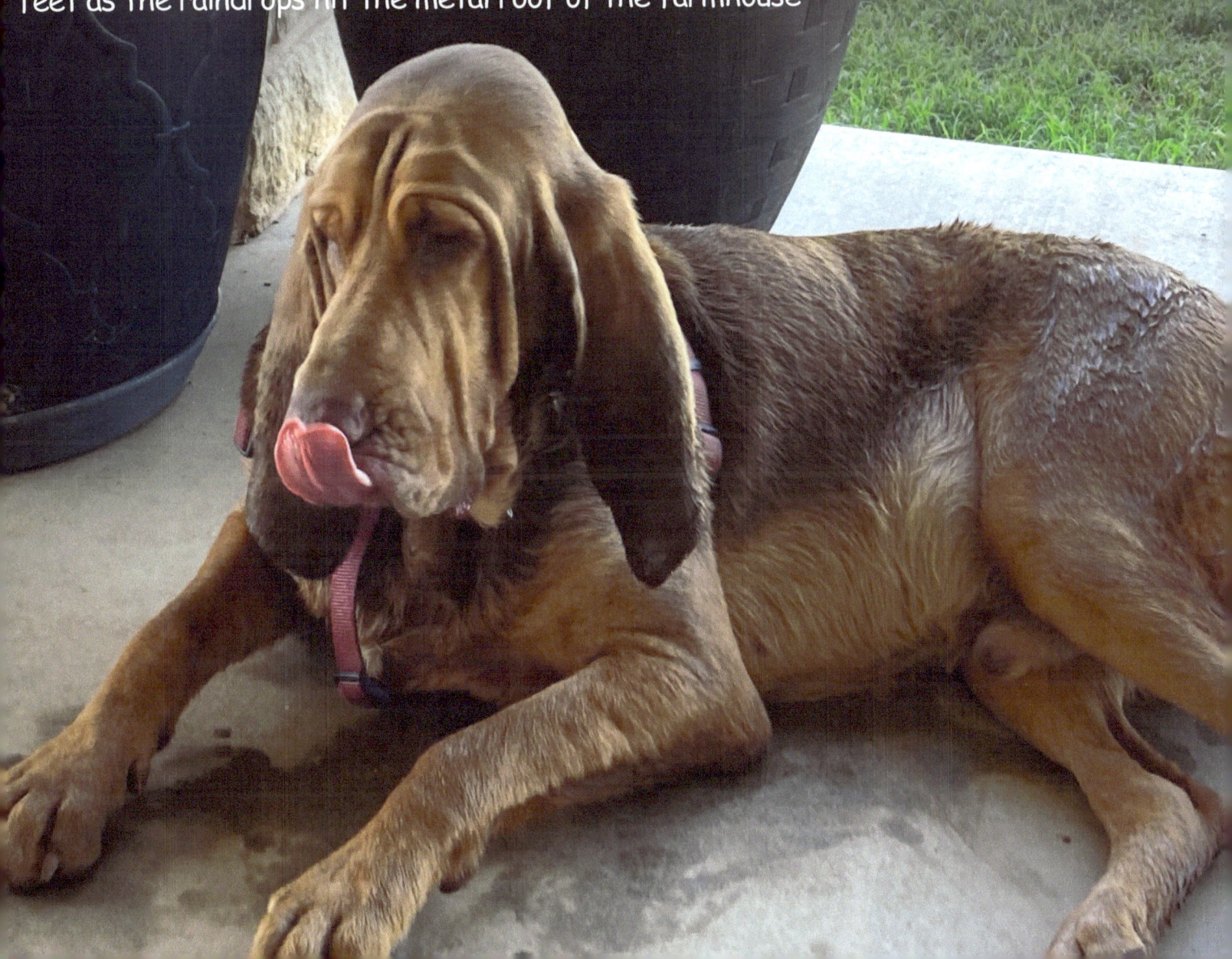

After a while, she would rise and say, "Let's go." I knew that meant we were going to our beds in the laundry room. We were never left outside in storms or in hot or cold weather. They always take good care of me and Scout.

One day, I decided to go out and see the baby calves. A Momma cow rolled me three times before I could leave the pasture. Momma was upset. She thought I was hurt. "That's the only way he is going to learn," Daddy said.

I don't like the cattle to get close to Momma. Daddy walked around them all the time but Momma only went close to them when she was helping Daddy feed or work cattle.

Momma was working in her vegetable tanks. Some of the cattle came over to watch her. One of the black heifers poked her head through the steel fence. I nipped the heifer on the nose.

Momma scolded me, so I just sat down and glared at them. When I kept growling, she started laughing and said, "Buddy, they are not hurting me." I kept watching, just in case. Momma just doesn't understand. They are big. I have to protect her.

There are special people who come to the farm to visit. Momma and Daddy call them grandkids. I like them. They play with me. They rub my head and my belly. They run with me through the yard. They throw the tennis ball for Scout. And when Momma isn't looking, they give us treats.

There is always lots of food at the farm. Momma likes to cook. When people come for supper, Scout and I know there will be scraps for us to share.

I got to celebrate my first Christmas at the farm. They gave me a pretty red blanket to lay on.

I make Momma and Daddy laugh sometimes when I try to talk. When they rub my ears, I make noises that sound like talking. Sometimes, Daddy talks to me, and I try to talk back to him. One time, Momma and her friend were leaving the house. Daddy told me to say goodbye. I mumbled a lot of sounds. Everyone was laughing.

Another time, I tried to put my front paws on the kitchen cabinet. Momma said, "No!" I walked away, mumbling. "Don't sass me," she said. Momma's voice told me I needed to go lay down.

I chase rabbits through the yard and the pasture. They often run into a drainage pipe to hide. I sniff and growl but they don't come out.

I love the wheat pasture on the farm. Bloodhounds love to smell things. I like to go to the wheat field because Daddy plants turnips with the wheat. Cows love turnips. I don't eat them, but I like to smell them.

I love the barn where, on cold days, I curl up on the car mats Daddy laid in the corner for me and Scout. I have never lived where there is cold weather. I know the heat from the summers in south Texas, but not cold. On cold days, Momma let us sleep on our rugs in the laundry room. On really cold days, she let's us lay in front of the fireplace. I curl up beside Scout on a rug and fall asleep.

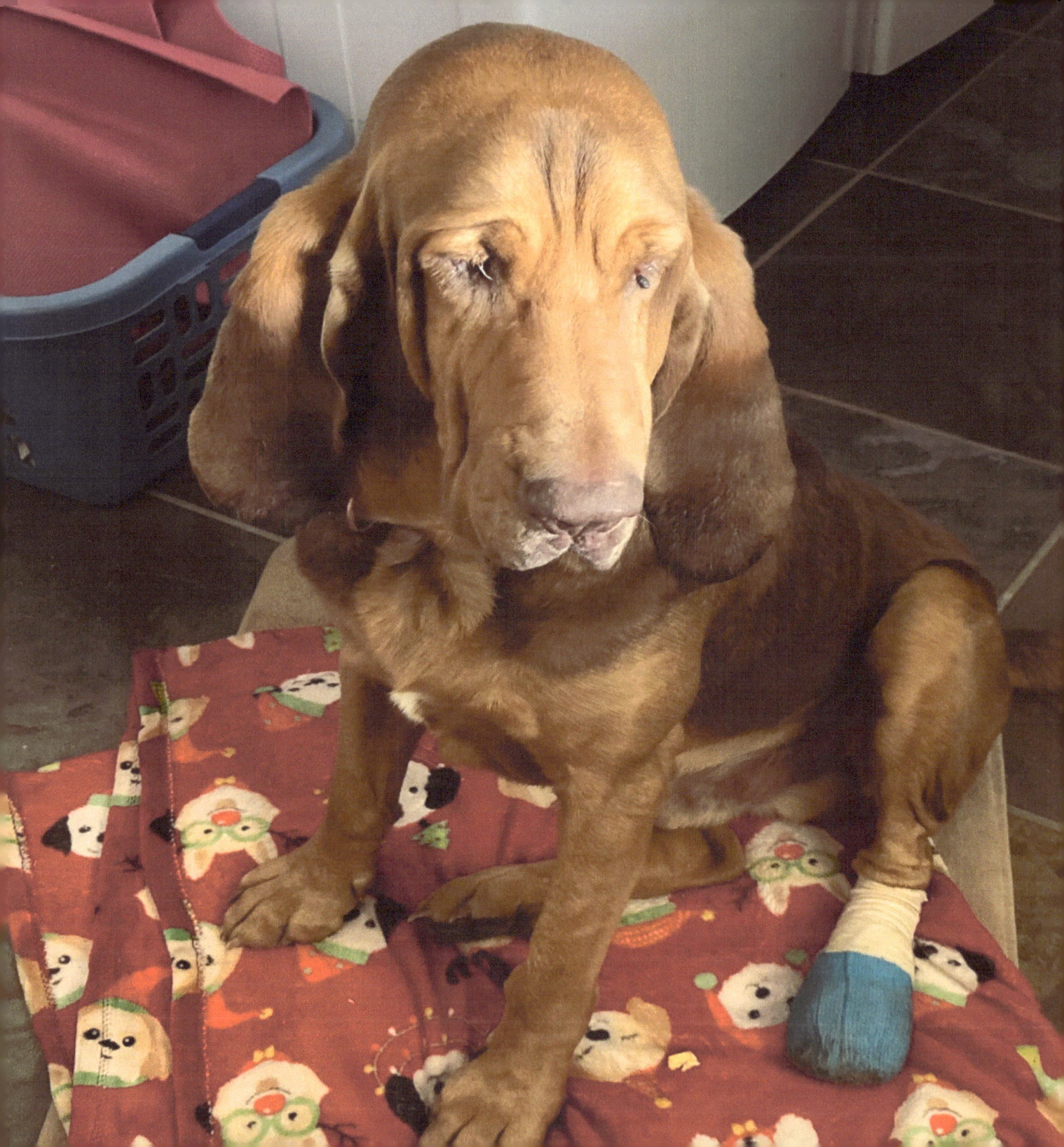

I love the farm. I love Scout. I love Momma and Daddy. I love the grandkids and the people who come to visit at the farm. I finally know what love means. I have people who care for me.

When I need to go to the veterinarian, they take me. One time, I cut my foot on some metal in the fence pile. I had to have surgery. When I came home, Momma and Daddy changed my bandage every day until I was well.

I have everything I ever wanted. I love it when Momma cooks roast and we get the leftovers. I love cooked carrots. They are one of my favorite foods. When people visit the farm, they sometimes ask to meet me and give me hugs.

I have rugs on the back porch, in the laundry room and in my doghouse.

I've had many adventures on the farm. My life here is exciting. There is so much to do! My favorite part is my family. Momma and Daddy love me. Scout plays and runs with me. We cuddle up together and take naps.

Life at the farm is good. Tomorrow there are new things to see and new places to go!

Buddy's version of "Where's Waldo?"

I can sleep anywhere.

I smell a rat in here!

Where did that raccoon go?

It is all eyes on Dad when it's time for treats.

Sometimes Momma has too much help in the garden.

Something is cooking in the kitchen

I see you little mouse

About the Author

LaDonna Wilkerson lives in southwest Oklahoma with her husband, Ed. They have lived in five states due to Ed's military service. They moved to 8B Farm after his retirement.

They were blessed to raise three sons – Abe, Zac and Caleb. They have eight grandchildren. LaDonna recently retired after 25 years as a bar-certified paralegal.

Her hobbies include traveling, reading, writing, gardening, quilting, painting barn quilts and cooking for her family and friends. She is an avid Oklahoma Sooner Softball fan.

Spending time with her grandchildren is her favorite way to have fun. She teaches Bible classes to PreK through fifth grade on Wednesday nights and coleads a card ministry for older women at her church.

www.ingramcontent.com/pod-product-compliance
Lightning Source LLC
Chambersburg PA
CBHW040020130526
44590CB00036B/36